FINAL THOUGHTS

Beginner's Guide to Death

Beginner's Guide to Death

FINAL THOUGHTS

FINAL THOUGHTS

Beginner's Guide to Death

A Thanatology Anthology
of Fables, Lyrics, Aphorisms,
Riddles, Rhyme and Reason

Mark Mathew Braunstein

Panacea Press
Quaker Hill, CT

Final Thoughts
© 2019 Mark Mathew Braunstein

Cover design by the author, aided by Adobe Photoshop.
Book design by the author, hindered by Adobe InDesign.

Panacea Press
P.O. Box 456
Quaker Hill, CT
06375-0456

BISAC Subject Headings:
HUM003000   HUMOR / Essays
PHI035000   PHILOSOPHY / Essays
REL085000   RELIGION / Eschatology
SEL010000   SELF-HELP / Death, Grief, Bereavement

Library of Congress Control Number: 2018966460

ISBN 978-0-9635663-6-2 (paperback)
ISBN 978-0-9635663-7-9 (e-book)

First (and likely Final) Edition: 2019
10 9 8 7 6 5 4 3 2 1

Dedicated to all those I have known in the past who have died and disappeared into Eternity but who might yet reappear in the future as Posterity, and so might open this slim book of slim logic to find themselves glimpsing this very text, perhaps to become blinded by the whiteness of the page that engulfs this seemingly endless sentence, or perhaps to become mesmerized by the tiny dot of blackness that concludes it, all while continuing to grapple with a contradictory awareness that death shares as much in common with a peripheral period that terminates a life sentence as with comatose commas and semiconscious semicolons that perpetuate the endless cycle of eternal return.

other books by the author:

Radical Vegetarianism: A Dialectic of Diet and Ethic
(1981, Revised Edition 2010)

Sprout Garden: Indoor Grower's Guide to Gourmet Sprouts
(1993, Revised Edition 1999, Spanish translation 2012)

Microgreen Garden: Indoor Grower's Guide to Gourmet Greens
(2013, Spanish translation 2019)

Good Girls on Bad Drugs: Addiction Nonfiction in a Revised Edition
(2017, Revised Edition 2019)

Some portions of this book were adapted from earlier versions first published in these books and magazines:

- Chapter 01: the "Being and Nothing" fable in *The Mystic Muse – Tales for the New Age*, Autumn 1987.
- Chapter 03: the "Jennifer" passage in *Good Girls on Bad Drugs*, 2017, Panacea Press revised edition 2019.
- Chapter 03: the "See You Later as an Alligator" passage in *Radical Vegetarianism*, 1981, Lantern Books revised edition 2010.
- Chapter 04: the "Rembrandt's Self-Portrait as Zeuxis" passage in *Iris – Notes in the History of Art*, December 1983.
- Chapter 06: the "Rynn Berry" eulogy in *Vegetarian Voice*, Spring 2014.
- Chapter 07: the "Walking to Our Graves" chapter in *Spirit of Change – Holistic New England*, Spring 2015.

Contents

Introduction
to a Thanatology Anthology

You need not have one foot in the grave in order to think about your grave. While society may diagnose me as being morbid to think so deeply about death as to also write about it, you must be equally morbid to dare to read about it. So, to distract us from advancing beyond this paragraph, who do we need more: a shrink, a cleric, a shaman, a miracle worker, a social worker, a sex worker, a bartender, a drug dealer, or an editor?

Lacking all of them, I am writing my thoughts about death to free my mind from those thoughts. If I so often am thinking about this nebulous concept of death, it is because death lurks everywhere around me. Shelley: "Death is here and death is there / Death is busy everywhere." And because everything presently living is concurrently dying.

Yet, today in our society, we observe a taboo about speaking openly about death. If in middle age we shy away from divulging our age, it may be because aging is our undressed rehearsal in preparation for dying. So we do not speak of dying anymore. Instead, we say we merely pass away. We leave behind no corpses anymore. Instead, we remain bodies. No brothers die before their sisters anymore. Instead, sisters are predeceased by their brothers. We no longer are laid out in coffins by undertakers anymore. Instead, we are set to rest in caskets in funeral homes. We are not buried in graveyards anymore. Instead, we are interred in cemeteries. People are not long dead anymore. Instead, they are "the late." Until we die, we do not compile our casket lists. Instead, we compile our bucket lists. Few of us still living cross off from our bucket lists our having read thick books about death anymore. Instead, we watch three-minute online videos about how to live forever.

If your oncologist or palliative care doctor informed you that you had only one day left to live, that beginning today you have no tomorrow, you probably would stop reading this page, would cast aside this book, and would run for your life. How about a year left to live? Would you still be reading? Either way, I'm sorry to see you go.

With no one now reading, now not even you, I am free to pound out on my keyboard these forethoughts, never to be chiseled into marble or granite, while I ponder some greater tome too lengthy for my tombstone. But do not think I yearn to crawl into my grave just yet. I still have things to do, places to go, people to meet, books to read, empires to build, worlds to conquer. And don't forget, advanced death directives and last wills to write. To be able to contemplate death is reason enough for me to cling to my possibly few remaining years of life. Because, once dead, I may no longer be able to ruminate upon birth and death and every one of life's stages in between.

When an infant is born, the first thing it does is cry or fall asleep or cry itself to sleep. The sleep of death is a work in progress in every wakeful moment upon life's way. Little wonder that I have been thinking about death all my adult life. I probably was thinking about it on the day I was born. I certainly will be thinking about it on the day that I die. So I will cease thinking about it only when I cease living. Meanwhile, my inscribing my thoughts about death has been a joyous time for me because thinking about death reminds me that I am so very much alive. I hope only to spread my joy and good cheer.

I am happy to be alive. I will be happy to die. Nothing really bad can happen to me if the worst that can happen to me is death.

Perhaps contemplating the concept of death while still living is as absurd as thinking about the meaning of the word "unthinkable." Perhaps I should wait until I have experienced death not merely secondhand but first. Until rigor mortis creeps through a dead body, I might prop it up to sit, but I can't make it talk. I can't make it reveal the answer to the riddle, "What is death?" So, no, I can't wait. I must inscribe my thoughts right now, prematurely, like an infant who is born too early, to avoid being stillborn.

Even though death will erase my thoughts, here in ink on paper or in pixels on monitor is what I think.

I think that Life speaks softly, like avowals of affection whispered into a lover's ear, enunciating slowly in broken phrases, taking a lifetime to spill its secrets to an impatient audience assembled in an overcrowded stadium. But the roar of the crowd and the echoes of the stadium drown out those whispers.

In contrast, Death speaks of its transgressions freely and boldly, but Death sits in solitude, trapped in an otherwise empty confessional whose door is locked and whose only key lies buried in a coffin. No priest or nun or choirboy or congregant can unlock the stall from the outside, so no one hears Death's darkest secrets spoken inside.

Death is a topic of morbid fascination that we may eventually outgrow but will never outlive. Death is my second favorite subject to read and to write about. Life is my first favorite. So, someday before we die, might you who reads many books about life also dare to read just one about death? If so, please allow me to whisper into your ear my own musings about this mysterious phenomenon that we call death, and I will keep on whispering until the day that death calls upon us. Are you ready?

If so, take your time, same as I have taken mine. Our only deadlines are our lifetimes.

Chapter 01

Parables and Fables

Chapter 01

Parables and Fables

about Paradoxes and Foibles

The Rock of Ages Rocked by the Ages of Rocks

On an immense rock upon a shore someone had inscribed: "Love will make you forget Death."

This spot became a favorite meeting place for lovers because they believed it, and so during many dawns arm in arm they watched the sunrise there while they forgot about death.

Then beneath that single sentence, someone scribbled another: "Death will make you forget Love."

After that, few people visited that rock anymore. Those solitaries who did venture forth were the unrequited and the betrayed, the suicidal and the forlorn, and the widowed and the divorced. Because they believed in nothing, they watched the sunset there while they hoped to forget about love.

Then one day, both inscriptions disappeared. Either the sea had washed the graffiti off the rock, or the rock had washed away into the sea.

Once We Go to Celebrate Two Wed,
Twice We Go to View Each Dead

The wedding procession: the limo and cars depart from the church so their occupants can reassemble at the banquet hall to celebrate the beloved newlyweds.

The funeral procession: the hearse and cars depart from the funeral home so their occupants can reassemble at the cemetery to bury the beloved deceased.

The two processions converge at an intersection where a traffic light has gone on the blink. Who should yield to whom? Life to venerate the dead? Or Death to celebrate the living?

The two lead drivers emerge from the hearse and the limo in order to negotiate. "Age before beauty," advises the driver dressed in black, guided by solemnity.

"Leave the dead to bury the dead," says the driver dressed in white, primed for celebration.

Both fall silent and neither budges.

By ones and by twos, drivers and passengers, some dressed up in white, others decked out in black, all emerge from their cars and intermingle at the crossroads. Members of one procession recognize close friends and distant relatives among the other procession. Some shake hands, others share hugs. Some shout with joy, others cry in lamentation.

The children of the deceased were old friends of the bride's parents. They explain to the groom's parents their connection to the deceased. Both pairs of parents gaze reverently upon the coffin.

"Where is he going?" wonders the groom. The corpse, if he could answer, would whisper, "To my grave."

A cop arrives to disperse the traffic jam. Everyone except for the groom returns to their cars. Instead of into the limo carrying the bride, the groom enters the hearse transporting the corpse.

"Where are you going?" the dismayed bride shouts out the window as her limo departs.

The impetuous groom yells back, "I'm taking the shortcut."

Being and Nothing

Momma Earth and Poppa Sky had two twin sons born six minutes apart that they had considered naming Art and Reality. At the dinner table, the hippie parents might have told Art to shut up, to give Reality a chance to talk. Or they might have ordered Reality, the elder, to stop picking on Art, to pick on someone his own age.

Alternatively, they might have named the older son Time, and the younger Space, except that Spacey might have been ridiculed for his nickname. Or named the younger Life and the elder Death, except that the older son might have been ostracized and suffered social stigma.

Ultimately, the hippie couple decided on the names Being and Nothing. The teachings of Zen convinced them that "nothing" is a good thing. "My younger son is good for a nickel," Poppa later said of his boys, "but my older son is good for nothing." Hence their names befit them.

Years later, anticipating ecological collapse and the end of civilization, the parents instructed their teenage sons where to find the family fortune and heirlooms in the event that Momma and Poppa "disappeared."

"Your two grandfathers' gold watches, which never agreed on the time, are stashed inside the cookie jar. All our money is stuffed under our mattress. The deeds to our home and cemetery plots are filed in the lower cabinet of the bathroom vanity. And two extra sets of house keys are buried under the brown stone in the backyard."

When Being and Nothing had just turned thirty-three, Momma and Poppa made a trip to Europe to visit the old countries of their own immigrant mommas and poppas, something they had vowed to do someday before their deaths. On the return transatlantic flight, their jet crashed, and Momma and Poppa were lost at sea.

Learning of their deaths, Being wept and wept for weeks. Eventually he recovered from his mourning and cashed out his inheritance to embark upon a journey in search of a new life.

Learning of his parents' deaths, Nothing rejoiced that they had lived so long and so healthfully, and that they had died so quickly and painlessly. 'Better than rotting away in their beds for months like their own aged parents had done,' he thought. He added his cash to the watch in the cookie jar, and buried the jar in his Poppa's vacant grave. With his unearthed set of house keys, he took possession of the home in which he had been raised, locked himself inside, and became a recluse.

A year later, Being returned home and told Nothing about his journeys roaming the country. At first, Being had hitchhiked, but he grew weary of lonely drivers who sought his companionship to bore him with sad stories about their misunderstood lives, all which sounded the same. So he bought a motorbike, but while speeding through the landscape he soon grew lonely himself. So he bought a car and gave rides to hitchhikers, but soon tired of the quiet passengers who often just fell asleep in the back seat. He resolved to find a companion who could stir him awake by day and whom he could embrace at night.

So Being settled down in a small apartment in the Big City to seek romance, at first in the singles bars. But those who easily fell into his arms at night as quickly slipped out the door before daybreak. So he resolved to find a woman who was ready to settle down and maybe even raise a family, but to prove himself worthy he himself needed to settle down. Hence his return to Nothing, sequestered in their childhood home.

Reunited, Being asked Nothing what had he done for the past year. "I was helping our father," Nothing answered.

"What was Poppa doing?" Being asked, puzzled.

"Nothing. Poppa is dead," he answered, his voice tinged with mirth. Realizing that Being did not get the joke, Nothing explained further.

While Being went searching for something worth searching for, Nothing did nothing while waiting for something worth waiting for. He stared intently into the mirror, waiting patiently for it to unveil his future. From one day to the next, he never saw the same face twice. With each successive gaze, that face grew older as he observed fleshy lines burrow semicircles under his eyes, his hairline slightly recede from his forehead, his sideburns reveal a touch of gray, and age spots surface on his cheeks. Every week and every month, that face was growing nearer to death. By the end of that year, he had ceased seeing his face in the mirror and saw only his death lurking within.

Not for a moment did Nothing's hermitage make him depressed. Quite the contrary, he was delighted by his revelations. He had never imagined that he would live long enough to bear witness to his face being sculpted and shaped by the passage of time. And he understood that while we all were condemned to die, we all were granted reprieves to live a full life until we died. End of story. Then Nothing fell silent.

"How might we live a full life?" Being asked.

Nothing answered, "By preparing for death."

Both brothers became pensive. Then Nothing broke their long silence.

"But how might we prepare for death?"

Being answered, "By living a full life."

Feed Thy Enemy Porridge, Not Poison

An old proverb warns that hating your enemy is akin to taking poison and hoping it will kill him. Actually it is just as foolish to hope to kill your enemy. Why put him out of his misery? Better to let him live long enough to suffer the indignities of old age. Let him become crippled by arthritis and stroke. Let him suffer the pain of fractures and cancer. Let him witness the deaths of all his friends and family ahead of him. Let him die alone with no one to comfort him in his dying and no one to mourn his death. Let him experience aphonia and aphasia. Let him drool and become bedridden and wear diapers and lie in a pool of his pee and poop. Let him die out of boredom of the same old shit.

Digging His Own Grave

The jogger jogs. What is she running from? From boredom and its eventual sloth? From decadence and its consequential obesity? From aging and its incipient debility? From life and its inevitable death?

The athlete had taken utmost care of her body, had run five miles daily, had never smoked cigs or drank booze, and had eschewed white sugar and white flour and red meat. Now, she had lived to a ripe old age, outlived most of her ever-dwindling circle of friends, and seen them all crawl crippled into their graves. Her favorite pastime was visiting all of her old friends in their graves. Reading the dates on other tombstones in the vast, seemingly endless graveyard, she discovered that, for most of the elderly husbands and wives buried side by side, one very soon followed the other to the grave. The first may have died from a weak heart. The second surely had died from a broken heart.

An old gravedigger with a weak heart has died, his backbreaking labors over the graves he previously had dug for others having contributed to sending him to a grave of his own. So a young gravedigger is digging a grave for the old gravedigger, though knowing the digging will contribute to stressing his own heart.

While visiting the grave of a friend, the athlete asks, "What are you doing?"

The younger but wiser gravedigger answers, "Digging my own grave."

Panned Parenthood

When we were children, our parents told us, "When you have your own children..." and, "When your own children grow up..." and, "Wait until you have children." And our parents were told it by their parents. But where are the parents who do not tell that to their children, who do not indoctrinate their children to have children of their own? Speak up, you parents, speak up!

Your urge to bear children was driven by your innate desire to cheat death. You, the parents who consulted each other about your children's births, never consulted your children, never asked your children if they were weary of their world of the unborn. Instead you thrust life upon them like a bribe slipped into their empty pockets to buy them off, like a nipple stuffed into their crying mouths to shut them up. Your unborn were happy not knowing, not caring, not being. Your unborn never asked for the here and now but are here now and so they stay.

While you count your children, your children count their days. While you plan your families, your children plot their graves.

No Better Minute than the Last Minute
Allow me to introduce myself.

I am the last person that you want to meet. In fact, I am the last person that you *do* meet. I have anticipated meeting you since the day you were born and have waited patiently for that day when you will die. Perhaps unbeknown to you, I have always been by your side, even your bedside while you slept. I have grown with you and within you. All this time, I have been playing with you, like a cat with its half-dead prey. I have played the many roles of your lovers. I have acted in several roles as your children. Everything you have accomplished in life, you owe to me.

Because your name is Life and mine is Death. Had you not been destined for your one tombstone, you would never have bothered to reach your many milestones.

And yet, and yet. You still engage in the crime of squandering time, a crime for which you will be caught red-handed and so will plead guilty as charged. The sentence is life without parole, concluded by a death sentence. If, on the other hand, you lived forever, you would squander every minute, and life would hold less meaning for you. Adding meaning to life, death is a blessing. No greater incentive for accomplishment exists than waiting until the last minute, and no better minute than when you draw your last breath.

If you knew that you will die tomorrow, you could no longer continue pretending that you will live forever. So would you live like there is no tomorrow?

You wait all day long for something that never arrives. You search all night long for something that is never found. But every step forward is in the right direction because it is one step away from where you began. Regardless what direction, with every step you march toward death. Afraid of facing life, some turn to death. Afraid to face death, the rest simply cling to life. Regardless by what route, you soon enough will arrive at death's door that all along had been left open just for you.

Please remember to close the door behind you.

Standing Stillborn

Standing on a busy city streetcorner, we see two endless parades of human faces streaming by in opposite directions. One parade comprises those people we have known in the past, the other those presently unknown to us but who we may yet come to know. One group tugs at our memories, the other stirs our passions and inspires our dreams. On rare occasions, some people step out of that stream to ask us for directions. But we do not know where we are, and they do not know where they are going. So they quickly rejoin the parade and disappear into the crowd, which never disappears. Like a mighty river whose origin can be traced to a trickling mountain brook, the parade of faces from our past originates from the deep cavern of our birthplace. The parade of faces marching into the future empties into the vast pit of our gravesite.

The End of the Road

Life is a journey on an unfamiliar and dimly lit road, while death is a thick brick wall blocking further passage. Alert drivers with clear vision and antilock brakes can steer a detour around that wall and then continue on their life's path, while inattentive or drowsy drivers crash head-on, usually fatally.

The wall does serve a purpose more noble than mere obstruction. The Rosetta Stone that provides the code to unlock the secrets to the meaning of our lives lurks on its other side, so to protect that Stone from being damaged by careless drivers is the reason that the wall was erected.

In our rush to swerve around that wall, we all reach the end of our roads, usually by running out of gas. To attempt to grab hold of that Stone, some of us resort to prayer or to meditation or to yoga or to chanting or to fasting or to studying the holy books of all the world religions. Others develop the rare insight to simply slow down, to pull over, to exit our vehicles, and to walk around the wall.

The Hostess at the Hospice

We are all patients in hospice care. What line can be drawn between the terminally ill who will die in a month or a year and the rest of us who will die in ten years or fifty? We all fall ill. And, if we grow old enough, we all become crippled. The males, decrepit old men. The females, little old ladies. Born with expiration dates stamped on our rumps, young or old, male or female, we all will die.

With the smell of death on our breath, our last breath may not come with our next breath, but it will come. Death, that once-in-a-lifetime experience, awaits us regardless of whether we wait on a bed inside a hospital ER unit or on a bench outside the ER unit in its waiting room. It will come regardless of whether we sit in an armchair or in a wheelchair or in an electric chair.

The Salvation Armed Me

Though I have desired many things, I all along expected nothing and so expected all my desires to come to nothing. Hence, the little that I have been granted was more than I deserved. Neither a Buddhist who desires nothing nor a Christian who yearns for salvation, I aspire to be a wise man who lives happily, even if in hell, until he dies happily, even if banished from heaven.

Thus I went in search of Life. Along the way, I met Death.

"What are you doing?" Death asked me.

"Looking for Life," I answered.

"He went that away," Death said, pointing a finger at me, at which point Death turned around and walked away.

Grown elderly and weary of Life, I then went in search of Death. Along the way, I met Life.

"What are you doing?" Life asked me.

"Looking for Death," I answered.

"He went that away," Life said, pointing a gun at me, at which point I turned around and passed away.

The Bookmark in the Book of Life

When she first learned how to read, she began reading a thick tome intended for adults. At first, she struggled yet persevered. The book seemed so long that she doubted either she or anyone else could ever finish reading it. She placed a bookmark to indicate the page to where she had read.

As she matured, her reading skills improved, and her speed and comprehension increased. Protruding beyond the top edges of the pages, her bookmark slowly advanced towards the middle of the book. As more years passed and she read more pages, that bookmark still seemed stuck somewhere in the middle, holding the promise of still more pages ahead of her. This continued for years, as the final half of the book remained ever more elusive and ever more unread. At first, she thought it peculiar that no matter how many pages she left behind, just as many pages awaited ahead. Eventually, she no longer noticed. The strange became the norm. The norm became forgotten.

Then after a lifetime of her reading this same, seemingly endless book, quite suddenly that bookmark leaped from the middle of the book to its back pages. Perhaps a veil of unconscious denial had shielded her eyes, and now it had fallen from her face. Or perhaps the cataracts of old age had clouded her vision. Or perhaps her eyesight, sharply focused on the book, had grown dim to the bookmark. When her eyesight was restored as if with a flash of lightning, only then did she realize not only where she was in the book but where the book had been taking her all along.

When she finally finished reading and closed that book, she thought what a quick read it turned out to be after all, especially its last half. Then she flipped to the back cover to read the blurbs and endorsements. There were none. There was only the title. While on its front cover the title was *The Book of Life*, on its back cover the title over the course of many years had been revised and the tome had metamorphosed into *The Book of Death*.

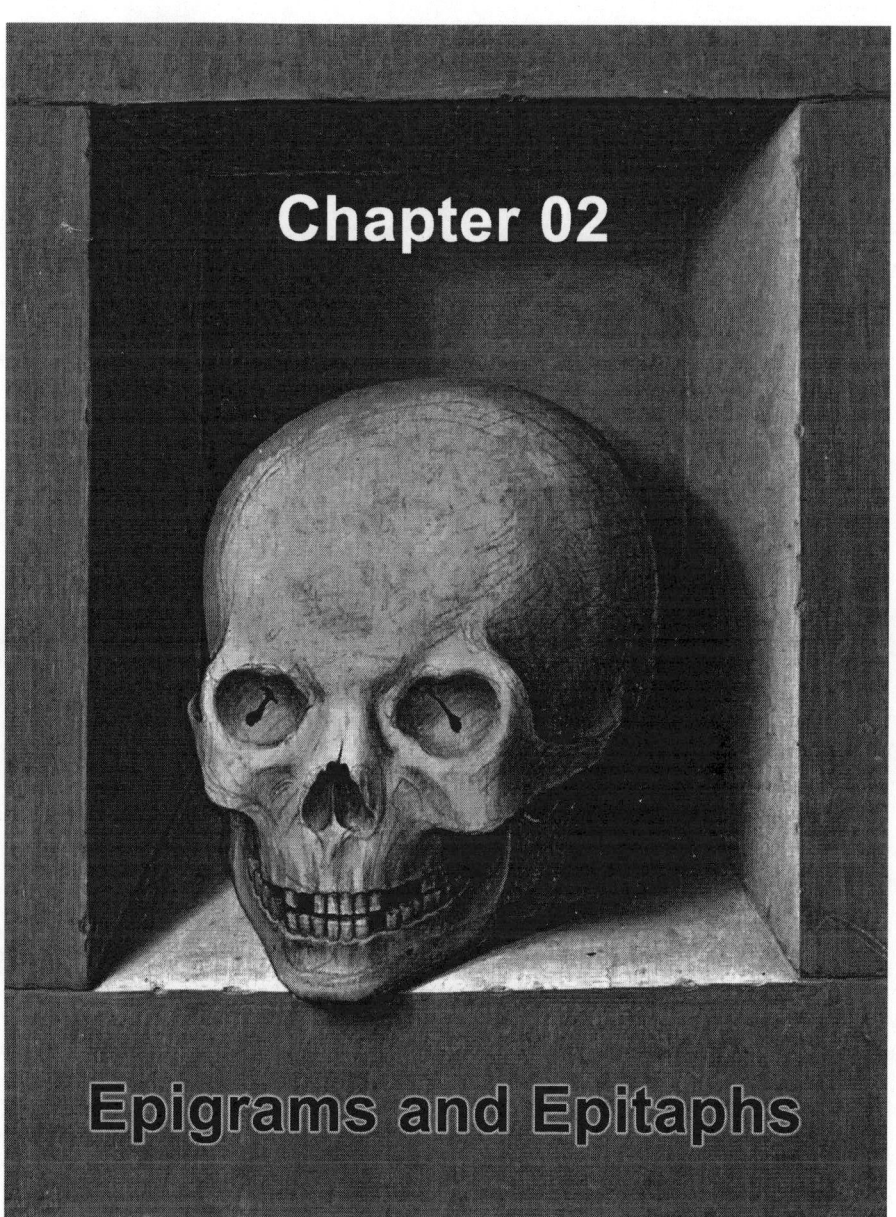

Chapter 02

Epigrams and Epitaphs

Chapter 02

Epigrams and Epitaphs

As Life Is a Joke, so Death Is Its Laughter

Sung to the tune of "Happy Birthday":
    Happy Birthday to me.
    Quite soon I'll be free.
    Every year brings me nearer,
    When I'm buried at sea.

Sung to the tune of "Happy Birthday":
    Happy Birthday to you.
    You're no longer new.
    Every year brings you nearer,
    When soon you'll be thru.

30

An outgoing voicemail message:
>   "This is the voice of my present, which to you is my past.
>   This is the voice of the ghost in the machine.
>   The ghost is asleep, dreaming about death.
>   The machine is dead, dreaming about life.
>   You who are awake may speak a message to posterity,
>   which shall be heard in eternity."

An outgoing answering-machine message:
>   "Despite this answering machine,
>   thousands of calls later my questions remain unanswered.
>   I'll ask one last time.
>   What is Life?
>   And what is Death?
>   Are we angels who have lost our wings,
>   Apes who have lost our hair,
>   Or apes who have lost our angels?
>   And least but not last, who am I?
>   And last but not least, who are you?"

An announcement on citywide outdoor loudspeakers:
>   "This is a test of the Nuclear Regulatory Commission's
>   emergency broadcast system. This is only a test. If this were
>   a real nuclear emergency, you would not be listening to this
>   broadcast. You would be dead."

Consumer beware:
>   Microgreens and sprouted mung
>   and gluten-free bread
>   will make you live so long,
>   you'll wish you were dead.

Principium moriendi natalis est. Dying begins at birth. *Principium est finis.* In the beginning, awaits the end. Inside the cradle lies a coffin. Tailgating the baby carriage is the hearse. Within every voluptuous body lurks the skeleton.

If our spirituality is measurable in inverse proportion to all the possessions that we have amassed, then we ascend to the pinnacle of enlightenment when we leave it all behind and die.

Life is cyclical in the same way that the Earth is round. Traveling a straight path will return you to the same place where you began. To fear death is to fear birth and, therefore, life. Those we know will die ahead of us or we will die ahead of them. Death should come as no surprise. Expressed in colloquialism "Get used to it."

Life is lived day by day the way that pinball is played game by game. The winner's prize is merely another game. The survivor's reward is merely another day. The winner is duped into playing until the game that she loses. The survivor is compelled to live until the day that she dies.

At class reunions, we view the march of time etched upon the faces of our former classmates, most who have grown to look as old as our own parents did when we were youthful students. At their fiftieth high school reunion, all the classmates had the same shocking news to share. During their recent annual physical exams, their doctors informed them that they all had less than twenty years left to live.

Day by day, we awaken, shower, scarf down breakfast, shuffle off to work, work, gulp down lunch, work, some more head home, have dinner, watch a video, and read ourselves to sleep. Year by year, we get born, learn to walk, grow up, go to school, learn to drive, go to college, learn a trade, get a job, get married, beget children, get divorced, get old, falter and stumble, stumble and fall, get injured and hospitalized, get buried and become forgotten. What did we learn?

Alive, we grope for the meaning of life, its meaning much like the snowflake that falls on our outstretched palm. Mysterious and beautiful, fragile and ephemeral, the snowflake immediately melts. Only when we are dying, as our hands turn icy cold, can we finally take hold of some flakes between our fingers, at which time we either grasp life's meaning, or we just stop groping.

Life is a gnawing problem to which we devote a lifetime whittling it down to a comprehensible size, but that is ultimately solved only by death.

Socrates said that the unexamined life is not worth living. "Nor is the unexamined death worth dying," said the doctor to the dying patient who was stretched out on the doctor's examination table.

What the hell is hell? Living hell is a life so painful and miserable that the afflicted commits suicide to end his pain and misery even though, as a Christian, he fears his suicide will condemn him to hell.

The best joke she ever heard:
    Q: What did the farmer say when his horse died?
    A: "That's funny. He never did that before."
    And she died laughing.

He was always in a hurry, yet he was always late. He was late even to his own wedding. He arrived on time only to his own funeral.

After the brief grief of painting herself into a corner, the abstract artist turned to painting landscapes. Her painting was a race between running out of paint and running out of canvas. Then, after putting everything into its proper perspective, she ran out of time and disappeared beyond the vanishing point.

All now alive will die, if not today, then tomorrow. Might as well buy your burial plot today, which is putting the coffin in front of the hearse.

People who lie in glass coffins should never throw bones.

At birth, we are grandfathered into our coffins. So there's no point in devoting our lives to making tons of money, if all we will have to show for it is our burials in expensive coffins that are no longer visible even to our children who visit our graves.

Q: Why did the chicken cross the road?
   A: To get to the other side of life.

We are students in the course called Life, but because we die, we all flunk out. The suicide is a student so fearful of failing the course that he drops out.

Later in her life, she looked ten years younger than her age. Yet even when she was nine years old, her very odd mother told her that she looked ten years younger than her age.

She walks the tightrope of Life while Death shakes it. She is a tightrope walker, Death the tightrope shaker.

He grew weary of breathing, so welcomed that last breath and, with one last exhalation, sputtered out his famous last words, "I can't breathe."

An inmate on death row, strapped down to the gurney in his execution gas chamber, should be breathing a sigh of relief. Yet, though doomed, he still fights for his life even with his last breath.

The only two things certain in Life are Death and axes. —Henry VIII

Is Life the candle or its flame? Is dying the flame or its smolder? Is Death the smolder or the air, its oxygen consumed?

The subject heading of an email announcing someone's death usually states only so-and-so's name, nakedly and with no modifiers, or issues the warning: "Sad news." But when the dearly departed was ninety-nine years old and was of sound mind and healthy body until nearly the very end, that is "Happy news."

Doctor Death's appointment cards all come preprinted:
    "You *will* be unable to keep this appointment, so please cancel within
    24 hours so that your time on Earth may be given to someone else."

"Knock, knock."
    "Who's there?"
    "Death."
    [*"The rest is silence."*]

This is a Death sentence.

Someone always is dying, yet he always is laughing. During his once-in-a-lifetime death experience, he will laugh especially hard and die laughing..

In the game of tug of war between Life and Death, Life struggles in its losing battle to pull Death over the line temporarily demarcating the two. Ever sympathetic to the underdog, you can add your muscle to the losing side of Life but should place your bets on the winning side of Death.

Birth: rising from less than nothing, to nothing.
    Life: gone today, gone tomorrow.
    Death: easier dead than done.

In the game of hide and seek, we the living run to find a place to hide from the irreversibility of time. Yet without even bothering to seek us, Death always finds us.

As a little boy, whenever he passed a cemetery, he thought to himself, 'That's where I want to live when I grow up.'

The armed bandit mugs a woman in a dark alley. He demands her wallet, so she removes it from her purse and hands it to him. He demands her ring, so she removes it from her finger and hands it to him. He demands her watch. "Oh, please," she pleads, "the last thing my grandmother did on her deathbed was hand me this watch." Taking a hint, he shoots the woman dead, and he removes the watch from her wrist.

Life is a book written in a dead language that no one speaks any longer, so the book remains unopened and unread, and its potential readers all die no wiser than when they were born.

An only child became a single mom who died during her only childbirth. Her son then grew into an adult who neither married nor sired any children, and who aged into an elderly man who outlived all of his friends. As an only child of an only child, he more than any seventh son of a seventh son can fully grasp the ephemerality of life and the inevitability of death.

Death is a forthcoming book of existential philosophy announced years ahead of publication and waitlisted at the library and backordered at the bookstore. While awaiting its release its eager audience instead reads fairy tales and comic books just to retain their reading skills, but by the time that book wanders into print, its anticipation has been forgotten, and everyone dies happily ever after.

Chapter 03

Real-Life Dialogs with Death

Chapter 03

Real-Life Dialogs with Death

Cryptic True Tales of the Crypt

As a ten-year-old child, I often tended to birds that were stunned after they had flown into windowpanes in which they saw mirrored the forest behind them. Until they regained consciousness, I guarded them from predators. Sometimes I placed them into darkened boxes, other times I simply watched over them where they had fallen.

One bird, a northern flicker, the most beautiful of any bird that ever struck my windows, struck me with its beauty, all the more apparent when inspected up close. As I cradled it in my hands, its breath quickened, its heart pounded, and then . . . stillness and silence. Its dead body rested in my hands while, perhaps, something ineffable flew away and crashed through some other distant window as through Alice's looking glass.

As my second visitation by Death, this became a defining moment in my life. Now, whenever I look into the mirror, I am reminded that I am gazing into the face of Death because, since last time I looked, I had grown older, and so, hour by hour and day by day, nearer to my death.

Thus the world behind the mirror reveals as many truths as the world in front. In front, the dream world of the living. Behind, the dream world of the reflected forest into which that flicker had flown away.

As a nine-year-old child, I did not see my first pet dying. Unlike that flicker whose life I beheld flickering away, Pokey's death occurred off-camera. One evening, the parakeet was as healthy and robust as ever, perching in her favorite corner of the cage, chirping at and transfixed by the "other" parakeet reflected in the toy mirror. Next morning, she lay dead on the floor of the cage.

My mother, who routinely gutted dead chickens and annually stuffed a dead turkey so that we might bury them in our stomachs, nevertheless cringed at the thought of handling the body of this tiny, fluffy parakeet. So she implored me to remove Pokey from her cage and to bury her in our yard. I did both with equanimity. My mom still viewed Pokey as a family pet. I now viewed Pokey as only a handful of ruffled feathers with a faintly familiar face.

Yet, as my first visitation by death, the sight of Pokey's body lying on the cage floor still haunts me. That little boy wondered, 'Pokey, where did you go?' Perhaps Pokey joined her "other" in the mirror and, together at last, they both then flew away.

Jennifer was a heroin addict and a sex worker whose honesty and integrity shined amid all the lowlifes with whom she shared her dark underworlds of addiction and prostitution. Unashamed to admit that I had made her acquaintance, I am heartened to know that, for now, she appears to have made her escape from the streets.

But she has made no such escape from drugs. She swapped her addiction to heroin for addiction to methadone. Unlike methadone, heroin is infused with a secret sauce called "death wish."

Drugs and alcohol are anodynes for addicts who are dispirited and disheartened, but too cowardly to kill themselves, so they abuse some substance in hopes that it will end their lives for them. Each track mark memorializes a botched stab at suicide. After many failed attempts of reaching for the sun, the heroin addict overdoses and, like Icarus, plummets to Earth.

Just as a mother's love is boundless, so can her sorrow be endless. If there exists a wailing louder and deeper than her mourning over her child's death, it is her grieving its suicide. Her child's willful renunciation of her gift of life is a wound from which no mother can heal.

Jennifer's son had followed her descent into drugs. At age twenty-two, he added his corpse to the body count of the opioid dead, mostly fueled by heroin laced with fentanyl. His death certificate documented that fatal brew as "Acute intoxication from the combined effects of Fentanyl, Heroin & Alcohol."

In the natural order of birth and life and death, the grandmother dies, then the mother dies, and then, years later, her son dies. But with drug addiction, life is backwards. When the son is a heroin addict, the son often dies first.

In contrast, my friend's teenage son, though not yet addicted, survived an overdose of an unknown opioid purchased over the Dark Web. He was left a quadriplegic paralyzed below the chin, unable to move any part of his body, but able to feel all of its pain. That is, able to feel pain when not heavily sedated. And unable to see or to speak, but able to hear and to open his mouth. Once to signify "yes," twice to signify "no."

Both loving parents devote more than half of their lives to sitting by his bedside in his hospital room while entertaining him by playing music and reading aloud. They prolong his dying by intervening medically, keeping their nearly half-dead son barely half-alive.

If I were the son, I would open my jaw twice and would never stop motioning twice. Twice, twice, twice. To signify to pull the plug on my many doctors' machines, and to my two parents' machinations aimed at perpetually suspending me in a near-endless stage of end of life.

Q: What is worse than becoming a quadriplegic heroin addict at twenty-two years old?

A: Becoming a quadriplegic heroin addict at twenty-two years old, and living to be ninety-nine years old.

Occasionally, I still listen to selections from my nostalgic collection of vinyl LP records. On my archaic manual turntable, I play the B side of Beethoven's C-sharp Minor Quartet, Opus 131, its final three movements of the seven-movement string quartet. I contemplate dying while the music plays and of releasing my last breath when the string instruments reach their finale. Until I lift the tonearm from the inner groove of the record, the stylus clicks repeatedly, echoing my heartbeat. Music to my ears as if the music of the spheres, that nearly endless clicking heralds the beckoning call of the eternity of death.

For eighteen years, Barbara had battled cancer, which had metastasized to half of her digestive and respiratory organs. As a fifty-five-year-old, she looked eighty-five. Nearing the end of her struggles, she appeared so ghostlike that only her pain marked her as human. At the conclusion of my visit, I gently spoke to her my parting words, "Death is beautiful. Dying is ugly, but death is beautiful." In response, she smiled, and as though singing a monosyllabic hymn, she whispered just one word, "Yay!" Four days later, she gave up the ghost.

Late night at the college pub, I, an art major, was deep in conversation with a classmate, a dance major. Emboldened by beer, sex may have been on her mind, as it was on mine. We shared our thoughts about thinking. I think she claimed that she was always thinking, except when dancing and except when making love. I think I replied that I, too, was always thinking, but I never danced, and that I did think while making art and did think while making love.

"What do you think about when making art?" she asked.

I answered, "I think about life."

"What do you think about when making love?" she asked.

I answered, "I think about death."

She then excused herself to go to the ladies' room and slipped away into the darkness.

When used to describe an old friend, the word "old" means either "elderly" or "longtime." And eventually both.

When I learn of the deaths of old friends and former acquaintances, for the next several days my memories of them haunt me. They may have last crossed my mind many years ago, but still my dim memories are reawakened. As we grow older, we receive that news with greater frequency. As time passes and fewer people our age remain alive, such news comes our way less often. With some luck, we will die before everyone we have ever known has died ahead of us.

A reason enough for living might be to keep the dead alive in our thoughts, and to keep alive all our other thoughts that will die with us.

Feminine beauty might be embodied in lengthy hair, a shapely figure, a graceful stride, befitting attire, and childlike facial features. Yet wait three decades, and all those attributes become history. A woman can fend off signs of aging by enlisting the joint services of a hairdresser, an athletic trainer, a yoga instructor, a custom tailor, a manicurist, and a makeup artist. Big bucks can call in the big guns of Botox injections, tummy tucks, breast implants, face lifts, chemical peels, hair removals, teeth whiteners, laser treatments, plastic surgery, liposuction, and incantation. Buffered by her body guards, a woman can turn back the minute hand of the clock so that her mirror reflects some past glory rather than her present decline. But such safeguards last barely minutes. A woman may briefly delay the tyranny of time, but none can escape it.

The youthful and middle-aged Greta Garbo had a face that many had idolized for its feminine perfection. But as she grew old, her beauty faded. While she hardly hid her face in shame, she did retreat from the public spotlight, if living in the middle of Manhattan can be described as retreating. Some say she did so to spare her admirers from being disappointed by the ephemerality of beauty. I think she did so to spare us from being shell-shocked by the mortality that dwells within us all, not to protect herself from us but to protect us from our deaths.

I knew the elderly Greta Garbo, albeit only casually and superficially. I worked in a health food store near the United Nations in the very posh neighborhood of the affluent Upper East Side of Manhattan where she lived in her retirement. Inconspicuously dressed in hiking boots, dungarees, and a ski coat in winter or an army jacket in spring and fall, she shopped once a week for a few select items, among them always Monterey Jack cheese. In the manner for which Manhattanites are well known and precisely for which celebrities seek residence in Manhattan, I did not ogle her, did not beg for an autograph, did not treat her deferentially in any way. Instead, I showed the same respect for her privacy that I did for any other customer's. For that matter, had Death come knocking on my health food store's door, I would have accorded the same due respect for the cloaked and hooded figure of Death whose celebrity status surpasses that of even Greta Garbo.

Indeed, while living in the middle of Manhattan, I was visited by Herr Death in a dream in which I was afloat in the air, just below the ceiling. I looked down into my bedroom and saw . . . myself, asleep on my bed. But some other occupant of the room was standing over me. It was Mr. Death, cloaked and with his face shielded by his hood. In my dream, I who was wakeful and floating tried to shriek, but my voice was dumbstruck. I awoke abruptly, sweating, feeling frightened.

Twenty years later, while living in the woodland of an arboretum, I again was visited in my dream by the archetypal figure of the old man Death. This second time, however, I stood before him and looked him straight into his gaping hood.

'Finally! I've been waiting for you all my life,' I thought. And then I said, "Let's go! I'm ready."

"No," he countered, in plain English, free of accent. "Not yet."

The wish to be cremated is often disregarded by those entrusted to carry out the death directives of the newly deceased. Instead, their survivors give them decent burials. Recognizing this, funeral homes offer cremation super saver deals when paid in advance because many of those cremations, which are nonrefundable, never occur. The investment, not the body, goes up in smoke.

Why put off to tomorrow what you can do today? And why place the burden upon someone else to do for you tomorrow what you can do for yourself today? So, four years ago, like Queequeg ordering the *Pequod*'s carpenter to build his coffin, I purchased such a cremator supersaver for $999, which even includes transporting my corpse to the crematorium. I am looking forward to the ride.

Same as his ungrateful son, my father had a schadenfreude-shaded sensibility. He saw justice in everyone's hardships, including his own, and mocked us all for our woes that he deemed we all deserved. But he tempered his ridicule with a self-deprecating sense of humor.

All life long, he was an avid reader of print media. While bedbound in the hospice, he lost interest in the news of the day so stopped reading newspapers and magazines. Instead, he turned his attention to the more enduring news of the decade, if not of the century. He continued reading books. When he died just four months short of his ninetieth birthday, he was reading *1,000 Places to See Before You Die*.

If I were too weak to walk and confined to my deathbed as a semiconscious corpse, what then might I be reading? I would hope to die while reading the chapter in Edward Abbey's *Desert Solitaire* titled, "The Dead Man of Grandview Point." There at Grandview Point, a tourist from New Jersey had the good fortune to die of thirst with the desert panorama as the last thing he saw before closing his eyes.

While on a distant road trip, en route I visited Indiana County, Pennsylvania, not to admire its nuclear power plant nor to worship at the feet of its James Stewart statue, but to pay homage to Edward Abbey, born in Indiana, PA and raised ten miles north in Home, PA. I so highly venerate his writings that, when he was still alive, he was my favorite living author. But he has been bumped down a few rungs, as he now holds court alongside my many favorite dead authors.

In Abbey's penultimate novel, *The Fool's Progress*, the protagonist, upon completing a cross-country trip, dies from an illness from which he had long been suffering. The novel is largely autobiographical. After reading it, I wrote Abbey a fan letter in which I expressed my fear that he, too, was suffering from a terminal illness. I wished him good health so that he could continue writing his books and so that I could continue reading them. He replied with a handwritten postcard mailed from Oracle, AZ, postmarked February 3, 1989, in which he thanked me for my "interesting letter" and he commented about an article I had published in the magazine *Backpacker* that I had shared with him.

Five weeks later, he succumbed to the terminal illness from which he had long been suffering.

I have read enough books about death to last a lifetime, enough to fill an entire bookshelf. Spying those books and reading their spines, my mother asked me, "Why do you have so many books about death?"

I answered, "Thirty books is not so many compared to the more than three-thousand books that I have read about life."

In the end, my death. But before yielding to the sleep of death, I dream about death. And the next morning, my thoughts about the meanings of those dreams. Then during my waking hours, my thoughts about death, like little mosquitoes on sleepless nights, are buzzing in my ears and intruding in my dreams, leaving question marks on my psyche itching to be answered. Then at bedtime, when some pray, I protest. I protest against the emptiness of existence without purpose, against the injustice of birth without consent, against the imposition of death without escape. And then, when I fall asleep, I stop protesting and start dreaming, including my dreaming about death.

At the northern tip of Israel, fighting was still spilling over one year after the Yom Kippur War. I had enlisted as a temporary kibbutz worker, called a "volunteer," most of whom were American. Volunteers lived and worked segregated from the wider community of kibbutzniks who mostly ignored us because of our being so transient.

No Zionist, I planned to sequester myself during the summer tourism season, and to embark on a European art pilgrimage in the fall. I asked to be placed in the north due to lack of other volunteers who had stronger urges than mine for self-preservation. I was promptly dispatched to the border kibbutz closest to Mount Hermon, from which shelling and gunfire distantly rang out every night. Arriving at Kibbutz Shamir, I was asked my work preference. Interested in bees, I asked for work in the apiary, where volunteers interacted with kibbutzniks. I was assured that as soon as there was a vacancy, which would be soon, I would be placed there. But until then, I was assigned to harvest fruit.

On the morning of my sixth day, I was alone in the orchards picking Seckel pears while I was perched atop a mechanical giraffe whose motor thrummed with a low rumble. I heard two very loud explosions. Just another day on the northern tip of Israel. Unalarmed, I continued picking pears until an armed kibbutznik located me, easy to do because of my giraffe's motorized hum. He ordered me to seek shelter in the bunkers with all the women, children, and other volunteers.

Inside the dark and dank bunker, we were informed of a Palestinian attack in-progress. Others became worried or frightened, trembled or cried. Unless the reek of urine always pervaded the bunker, I suspect someone peed in his pants. I was calmly intrigued by the scene because no one really knew what was going on. I had made a new acquaintance there, a Norwegian woman, and we relevantly, if irreverently, philosophized about life and death and living and dying.

After three hours, we emerged to learn that four Palestinians from the Golan Heights bordering Syria had been killed by the male kibbutzniks, all reserve soldiers who farmed in the fields with their guns always at hand. The first kibbutz outpost that the Palestinians had descended upon was the hillside apiary, where their explosives had decimated the apiary and killed its three workers, two kibbutzniks and one volunteer.

On my thirty-ninth birthday, I was hiking with friends along a river when we came upon a footbridge from which three local farmers were diving again and again. Sober but celebratory, I was a mile swimmer itching for a swim, so I stripped down to my underwear and joined them. But I did not land quite right. I made a big splash.

As I descended into the river, a flash of light, like lightning, brightened the water surrounding me. When I reached the bottom depth of my descent, I remained submerged as though burdened with weights tied to me. I kicked and stroked to swim to the surface of the water. Or so I thought. Actually, I was getting nowhere. Gasping for air, I surfaced at long last. But I could barely swim, and my back really hurt. Something was painfully wrong. But to fix it, first I needed to get out of the water.

My friends and fellow divers pulled me onto the ledge of the riverbank and laid me on my back. "Ooooh, that hurts!" So they rolled me onto my stomach. This was before the era of cellphones, so the divers, who knew the trail and the nearby towns, left to summon help. The trail from the river to the road was a mile long. From the trailhead to the nearest town was nine miles. The night fell fast. Two hours later, a rescue team led by a state trooper arrived with a backboard stretcher. By flashlight, they gently lifted me onto it. Fully conscious, I talked amicably with members of the rescue team and especially with the state trooper.

"What time is it?" I asked. "Is it nine o'clock?"

The state trooper shined his flashlight on his watch.

"Yes," he answered, half humoring me, "it's nine o'clock."

"Then at this very minute thirty-nine years ago, I emerged from one womb, and now I have returned into another."

Bullets ricochet off water. The impact of my dive shattered a vertebrae that injured my spinal cord. Diagnosis: paralysis. Not everywhere, just below the waist. Prognosis: paralysis. Not forever, just the rest of my life.

For the next three decades, I have engaged my crutches and wheelchair as my swords and my shield in my crusades to successfully right several societal wrongs. In fact, were I not very visibly crippled, I could not have gotten away with some of my histrionics and, until legalized, outright crimes. Once, I indeed was arrested, but in court the charges were dismissed.

Others might call the event of my spinal cord injury the worst day of my life and might deem paraplegia a fate worse than death.

I call it a fate worse than birth, and recall that day as my rebirthday.

I was seated in my car, parked directly under an inner-city streetlight. The July night was hot and humid, so to catch a breeze my window was rolled down. A punk kid shuffled up to my window, abruptly reached through, and pressed a steak knife to my chest.

"I want twenty dollars!" the young thug screamed, thunder in his voice.

"Sir, I will give you twenty dollars, but first please put that away."

"No! I want it now!"

We repeated this heated exchange twice more before I capitulated. I took out my wallet and removed a twenty-dollar bill.

"I want it all!" the crackhead shouted, spraying spit through his rotting teeth. The lowlife leprechaun grabbed my three other twenties, withdrew his knife, and briskly walked away, disappearing into the night.

Though my life was threatened, my feathers were unruffled. But that's not the punch line. Rather, his life was more endangered than mine.

In my car door, I harbored a concealed handgun, for which I held a state permit. But I let the scumbag flee, even if to mug another victim. I drove home feeling as though I were a merciful judge who had granted a stay of execution to an unrepentant criminal who otherwise would have been hanged at dawn.

Which will run out first? The ink in my pen, or the beat of my heart? It is a race between my reaching the end of this page and reaching the end of my life.

That ten-year-old child who had experienced a flicker die in his hand grew into a man who witnessed a deer die on his watch.

We co-conspirators were enjoying a hike in the woods with the added allure of the sabotage of a hunt. The blasts of our foghorns had scared a deer out of range of a bowhunter's arrow. Still aglow with pride for averting a kill in the nick of time, a half hour later we came upon the scene of three bowhunters, one whose arrow had impaled the neck of a fallen deer. The wound was not yet mortal.

"I think you're disgusting!" a sister saboteur brusquely blurted out.

Both sides lost their cools. Shouting erupted and a scuffle ensued. A hunter shoved someone to the ground. I stepped away from the altercation to silently crouch down to look the splayed-out doe in the eye to accompany her on her imminent journey. She lay quietly, eyeing me, and then, like with the flicker . . . stillness and silence. In my sleep, her uniocular eye still stares back at mine, like the eye of the universe that in eyeing me eyeing it in turn eyes itself.

As plant fiber spattered with streaks of black ink, these pages provide little by way of nutritional value, which is why we only read books rather than eat them. Having during the course of a lifetime read far too many books and eaten far too much food, I hope by now to have become a wise and well fed corpse.

As Prince Hamlet so poetically observed, we fatten animals to feed their bodies to ourselves, and we fatten ourselves to feed our bodies to the worms. I aspire to much nobler creatures than worms. No point in wasting good food. I would much prefer to be eaten by a large predator, ideally to be devoured alive by a grizzly bear. But absent of becoming fresh meat, I hope my survivors feed my body to the black vultures of Death Valley or to the timber wolves of the Yukon or to the alligators of the Everglades.

See you later as an alligator.

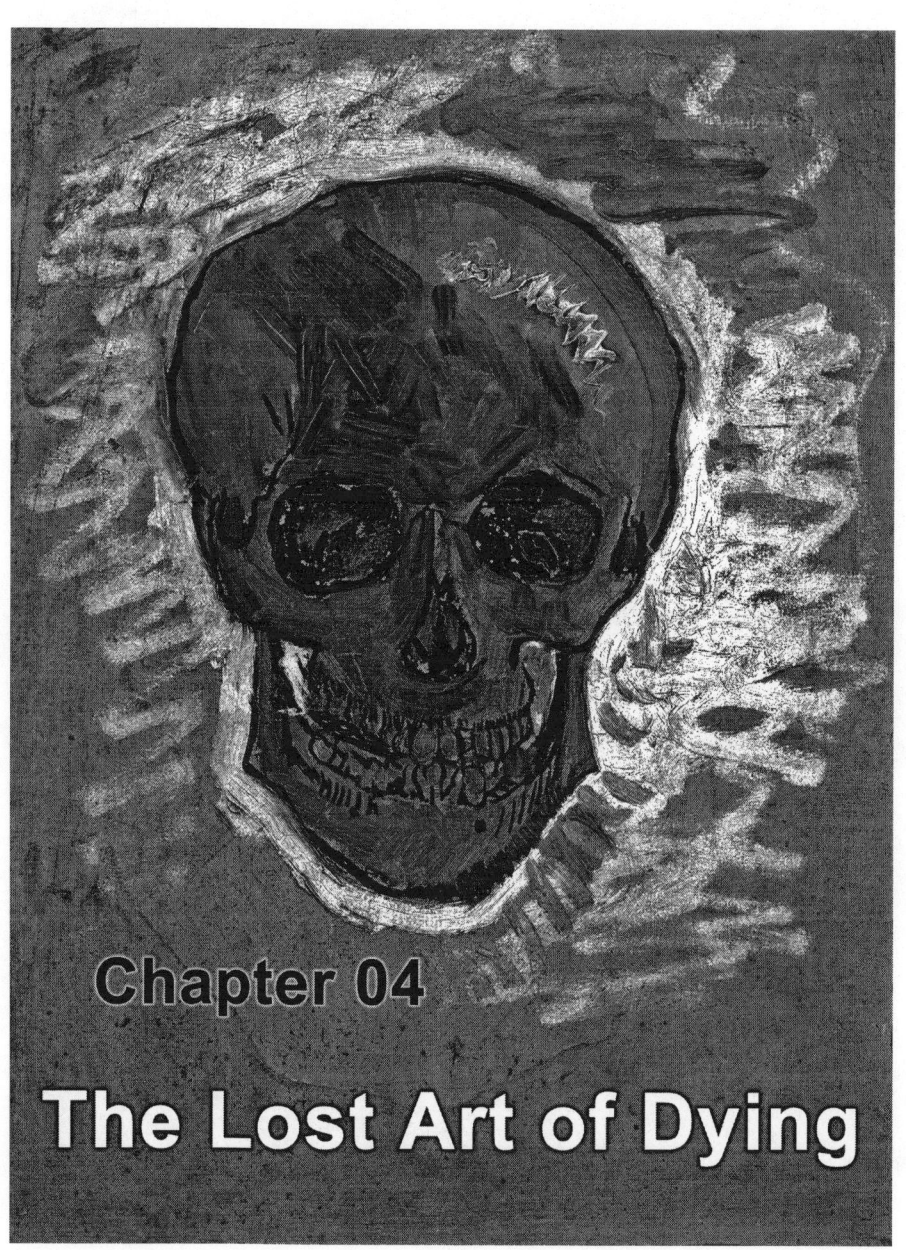

Chapter 04

The Lost Art of Dying

Chapter 04

The Lost Art of Dying

In Art as in Life (or is it the reverse?)

Jonathan Swift's *Gulliver's Travels* and Virgil's *Aeneid*
Swift describes the immortal Struldbruggs of the land of the Luggnaggians, who were doomed to eternal senility and infirmity because they could not die.

Apollo granted the sibyl of Cumae a year of life for each grain of sand as she held in her hand. But she was not so wise in her youth as when Virgil's Aeneas met her seven hundred years later, because she had neglected to ask for beauty and health along with her near-immortality.

She told the hero, "I want to die."

Left
half

Right
half

Lorado Taft's 1922 monumental sculpture **The Fountain of Time**

Perched on the southern edge of the University of Chicago's campus, this larger-than-life-size assembly of a hundred human figures marches in a procession from birth to death. It should more accurately be titled "The March of Time." The youngest lead the parade, while the eldest trail behind. Set apart from the march of the doomed stands a twenty-four-foot-tall statue of a solitary cloaked figure named Time.

Time stands still while watching the parade pass by. The sculpture illustrates lines from an Austin Dobson poem, *The Paradox of Time*, written in an archaic dialect. "Time goes, you say? Ah no! Alas, Time stays, we go." A more modern "translation":

> *Time marches on?*
> *No, Time stands still.*
> *Humanity marches on.*

Paul Gauguin's monumental mural of 1898

Describing it as a parable about birth, life, and death, Gauguin was suffering from syphilis and failing eyesight while struggling to complete this painting, his largest ever, after which he planned on poisoning himself with arsenic. But his attempted suicide was either feigned or failed. He was destined to wait five more years for the answers to the three questions posed by his painting's title:

Where do we come from? What are we? Where are we going?

*Rembrandt van Rijn's **Laughing Self-Portrait** of circa 1662-68*

The painter painted himself painting. Painting while laughing. Laughing at what? At himself? At the world? At Life? At Death?

He has lost his fortune, his fame, his home, his family and, surely the most devastating losses of all, his youth and his health. And yet he laughs. By the time he had completed this work, one-sixth of Amsterdam's population had perished in a plague, and still he laughed. While death is not a joke, neither is death a tragedy.

Life is a joke, and Death its laughter.

Percy Shelley's death poem of 1820

Death was on his mind and flowed from his pen throughout Percy Bysshe Shelley's brief life. He wrote a poem titled "Death" and another titled "To Death." His poem "Death Is Here and Death Is There," composed in 1820, expresses the most truths, though cloaked in archaic grammar that two centuries later may warrant our own revisions without any of our own additions. Such revisionism clarifies his two-centuries-old poem for our own mindset, and prepares his poetry for future generations, if any exist.

> Death is here and death is there,
> Death is busy everywhere,
> On all we are and all we feel,
> On all we know and all we fear,
>
> All things that we love and cherish,
> Like ourselves must fade and perish.
>
> First our pleasures die—and then
> Our hopes, and then our fears—and when
> These are dead, the debt is due,
> Dust claims dust—and we die too.

The best time to write about death is between midnight and dawn, so that the drowsy writer then can view the sunrise to reassure himself that he is still alive. The best time to read about death is between dusk and midnight, so that the reader can sleep on it and dream about death.

Because what we view or read just before falling asleep often resurfaces in our dreams, before going to sleep you might try rereading Shelley's poem, so that you might dream either about death or about his poem and thus fully grasp the meaning, if not of death, then at least of Shelley's poem about death.

Akira Kurosawa's 1952 film *Ikiru (To Live)*

A story of one man's simple search for some meaning to his life. The protagonist, dying of cancer, has vowed to accomplish something in his lifetime, which until then had been absent of anything meaningful. Bearing his cancer like Christ carrying the cross, he was resurrected to the tune of "Happy Birthday." So death spurred him on to fully live. Who of us is truly alive? Those who, if told they were to die tomorrow, would continue to live today exactly as they had lived yesterday.

Franz Kafka's 1925 novel *The Trial*

The book, though unfinished upon Kafka's death in 1924, does end with an execution. But that ending omits the final verdict as well as the trial itself. Rather, the parable, "Before the Law," contained in the chapter "In the Cathedral," offers closure. The chapter allegorizes the the tale of an alienated man tiptoeing through life. And the book serves as an analogy for the whole of life because, rather than provide us with any lasting conclusions or answers, life simply delivers us to death, as though life were but a Kafkaesque parable for death.

"Do not leave me!" implored Kafka on his deathbed. Kafka was assured by his bedside friend that he was not. leaving him. "No," countered Kafka, "but I am leaving you."

Marcel Proust's 1907 essay *Filial Sentiments of a Parricide*

The defining event in Proust's life was the death of his mother. "Ever since the death of my parents, I have become less myself and more their son." The Sun beams a message to Planet Earth: "Ever since the death of my *planets*, I have become less myself and more their *sun*."

John Ford's 1934 film *The Lost Patrol*

The colonel leading a British horse patrol in the Mesopotamian desert is keeping their mission "in his head." Then an unseen sniper shoots him in his head. His sergeant, Victor McLaglen, is left in command.

The sergeant asks his new second-in-command, "Do you know where we are? Do you know what we're here for? Do you know where we're going?"

"No," the soldier answers.

"Well, neither do I," McLaglen admits with a sigh.

The patrol takes refuge in a desert oasis where they hope to safely hideout but instead are killed one by one by more snipers. Boris Karloff, a shell-shocked and deranged private, believes the oasis is the lost Garden of Eden. Christlike, he tries to save his fellow soldiers' souls.

"You must have faith!" Karloff says, imploring the men.

"Why?" one of the soldiers asks. Karloff is struck speechless. No answer. Soon, while bearing a cross, Karloff is killed by a sniper.

Finally, only the sergeant and a private named Morales remain alive. McLaglen devises a plan that calls for them to separate so he can attack the snipers from behind. Morales does not agree, because he is afraid of dying alone. Instead, Morales, dazed by heatstroke, marches straight into the snipers' lines of fire. "Come back, Morales!" the sergeant screams. Morales is killed. Fulfilling his last wish, Morales was not left to die alone.

When Adam and Eve were exiled from eternal life in Eden, they were unafraid, knowing that at least one of them would not die alone.

The Music of the Spheres

Schubert's *Unfinished Symphony*, his eighth, would have been followed by his *Unbegun Symphony*, had he not composed his *Ninth Symphony*, past which few composers after Beethoven dared to venture.

Not even Beethoven could surpass Beethoven, so thereafter he concentrated on composing string quartets. The final movement of his final quartet, *Opus 135*, begins somberly, even ominously, posing the question, "Must it be?" He inscribed those words in German above the music on the score. In contrast to Charles Ives's orchestral and dissonant *The Unanswered Question*, Beethoven answered his query with a joyous outburst of strings and bows, exclaiming, "It must be!"

Beethoven was said to have sat up in his deathbed to shake his fist at the heavens unleashing a storm of thunder and lightning. He may have been interpreting in pantomime the two armored men's aria near the end of Mozart's final opera, *The Magic Flute*, first performed near the end of Mozart's life. "To conquer the fear of death is to ascend from earth into heaven." Yet Mozart may have feared his own death while composing his final work, a *Requiem*, upon realizing that it would commemorate not only the death of a count's wife, but also could glorify his own funeral. He died leaving his *Requiem* frightfully unfinished.

Bach, whose death preceded Mozart's and Beethoven's births, composed more than two-hundred cantatas, mostly religious, some secular, which is two-hundred more than we mortals deserve. The texts of his sacred cantatas often pontificate to trust in God in order to dwell in everlasting life and thereby to transcend death. For instance, the concluding chorale of BWV 26: "Who fears God shall live forever." Such sermonizing may have converted Christians into Lutherans, but surely failed in converting heathens into Christians. Fortuitously the texts are in German, so English speakers can concentrate on the music.

In his final composition, *The Art of the Fugue,* Bach embodied both the Beethoven shaken fist and the Mozart libretto maxim. While composing one of the variations of one of the fugues, Bach died, perhaps while seated at his harpsicord, still clutching quill pen in one hand and sheet music in the other. Thus this secular chamber work has no finale, no conclusive ending. Rather, like a sermon aborted in midsentence, it just ends in limbo.

"The rest is silence." A deathly silence with nary an angel plucking a harp. As the silence between the notes makes the music, all of Bach's Music of the Spheres concludes with the Silence of the Spheres.

Ingmar Bergman's 1958 film *The Magician*

A dying man is about to tell us what Death is. "Death is …," he mutters, and then he dies. The dead do speak from their graves. It is the living who, amid the cacophony of civilization upon the surface of the earth, cannot hear the muffled voices of those buried below it.

The unread *Orangutan Book of the Dead*

Living almost exclusively among other humans, we humans crowd out most other animals, especially wild animals, from our lives, from our thoughts, from our psyches, and therefore from our dreams. So when the Grim Reaper appears to us westerners in our dreams and in our art, it is in human or humanlike form. In contrast, indigenous tribes peoples who live in the natural world welcome into their dreamworlds as harbingers of death such animals as ravens, wolves, and orcas.

For twenty-six years, I shared my home in woods and meadows with several successive families of deer. The doe and her fawns admitted me into their families, and I regularly admitted deer into my wildest dreams. I learned to recognize each individual family member. I never saw one die or appear to be dying, despite their high mortality rates, But I certainly noticed when one went missing. That absentee likely was the deer who next appeared in my dreams.

As individuals, we humans must die in order to make room on the planet for those of our own species yet to be born. But as a species, we humans refuse to make room. Instead, the human race is crowding off of the planet all other species of plants and animals. When we think about the cycle of life and death, we humans think mostly about human life and human death, thus proving how little we understand about the web of Life.

We settle for the *Tibetan Book of the Dead* or the *Egyptian Book of the Dead* when we should be reading the *Orangutan Book of the Dead*.

Marcus Aurelius's second-century book *Meditations*

Echoing Socrates, Plato wrote in *Phaedo* that the purpose of philosophy is to teach us how to die. Socrates less emphatically said, "Those who practice philosophy practice dying." A collection of writings nearly as ancient as Plato's about how to live and how to die is Marcus Aurelius's.

In his honor, I dedicate my poem that I inscribe onto the blank first page of all the volumes of *Meditations* that I have bestowed or imposed upon friends:

Insincere Suicide Note #2 to My Future Self

Third-grade girls in pony tails
nicknamed me Marcus Aurelius.

Yet not till thirty-three and a third
did I open his little book,
which will outlast my little life.

When the cuckoo tick-tocks
my final five o'clock,
waste not good food.

Row me to the Glades,
feed me to the gators.

As you watch me disappear
through their teeth of time,
offer these pages as paper napkins
for their crocodile smiles.

Between passage from rebirth to redeath
these passages peruse,
so you on your deathbed
might lastly gasp,
"What, again?"

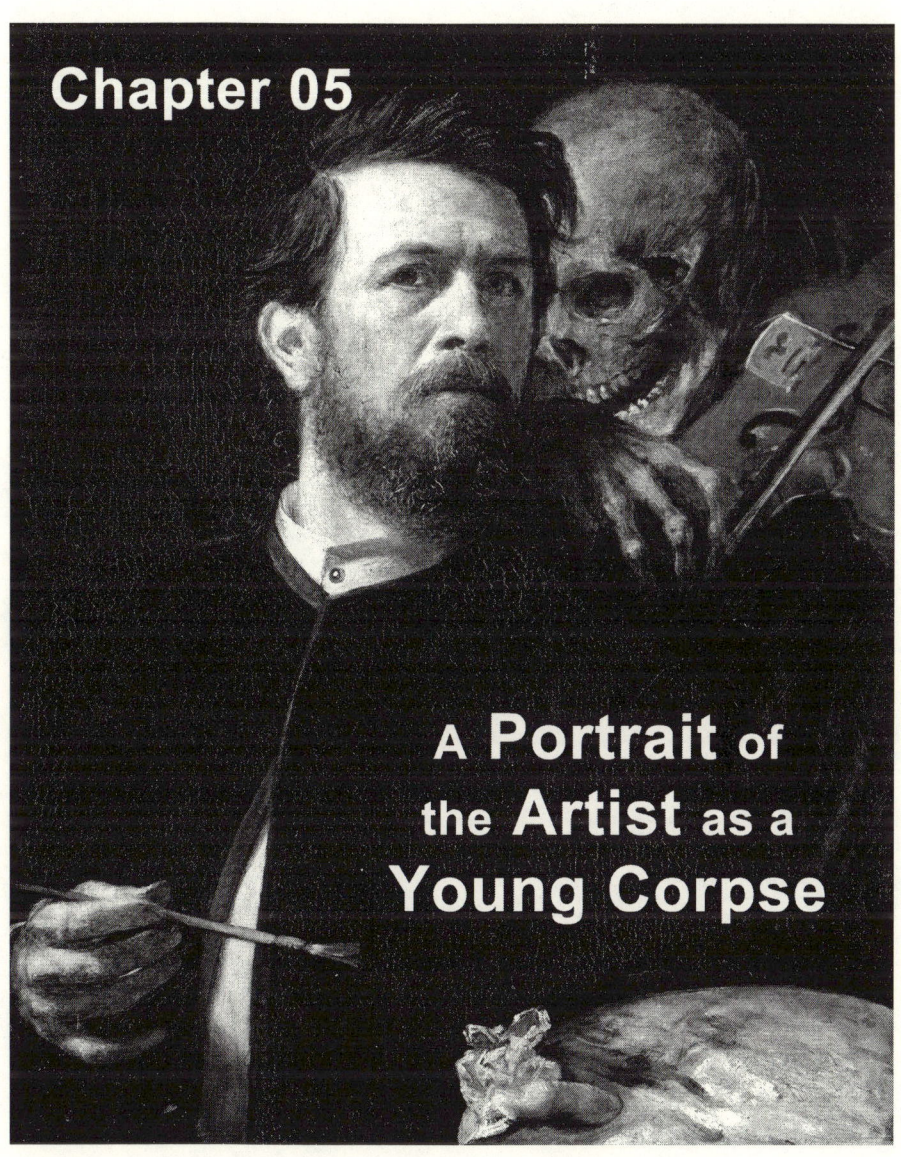

Chapter 05

A Portrait of
the Artist as a
Young Corpse

Chapter 05

A Portrait of the Artist as a Young Corpse

*Story without
a Beginning
or a Middle,
Just an End.*

[*Reader discretion is strongly advised.*]

Awaiting only a signature, the abstract painting was nearly completed. Its composition was a green starburst emanating from its yellow center outward to its blue edges. Buddhists and Hindus call that circular form a mandala, Christians and heathens call it a bull's-eye target. He had already painted several of these, but after this one he may have no need to paint another. He often had toyed with the idea of staring into its center long and hard in order to become mesmerized and disappear into it. Now he really did feel the need to escape.

In his mind's eye, all the paints on his palette were turning into black. Ivory black. Mars black. Bone black. Jet black. Carbon black. Ebony black. Everything was black. The blackness crept from palette to canvas, then from the canvas the darkness spread and enveloped the entire studio. In defiance of the intense overhead lighting, the entire room dimmed, like a movie screen at the final scene fading to black.

As a child, Arthur Kunstler had never been afraid of the bogeyman in the basement nor even of the dark in the night. Right now, though, he was struck with fear not only of the darkness inside his studio but also of the darkness inside his mind. He dreaded the blackness, wanted to purge it. His heart pounded, his pulse throbbed, and he grew short of breath. His chest heaved and brow sweated. He gritted his teeth. His father, when not sulking, had been prone to panic attacks, but until now that condition had skipped a generation. Or so he thought. Was Arthur indeed panicking? In desperation, he realized he needed to get out of there.

As he lumbered down the hallway that connected his studio with the bathroom, his leaden feet felt like they were dragging balls and chains. He flicked on the wall switch, but the ceiling lamp cast more shadow than light. Through the gloom, he squinted at the medicine cabinet mirror. Unwashed face and unkempt hair and untrimmed beard. He could do with a shower, but not now, not yet. He leaned forward, pressing his nose, then forehead, against the mirror's cold surface.

No entry.

He opened the cabinet door. Inside gleamed his metal razor, with removable blade, the old-fashioned kind his grandfather had used. No plastic throwaways for this bearded environmentalist, who rarely shaved anyway. He grabbed the razor and removed the double-edged blade. Barely used. Nice and sharp.

Arthur took a seat on the toilet lid. 'I've had enough. Just do it,' he thought. Do what? It, that's what. It. He primed himself to carry out this final act of courage. Or of cowardice.

"Need a pep talk," he said aloud, to no one. Or to everyone.

When the biology teacher pricked Arthur's finger with a pin to test for blood types in junior high, that was easy. Years later, he was challenged to prick his own finger to draw blood. Using the sterile scalpel supplied with a mail-in AIDS test kit, he pressed hard many times. No puncture. Then he stroked the scalpel along his forefinger. Not hard enough. Hard to do. He marveled how IV drug addicts could so casually pierce themselves several times daily when they shoot up.

Can a scorpion sting itself, even if only accidentally? Or is it immune to its own venom? Holding the razor blade poised over his left wrist, and with his left fist clenched, he sat still for two or three frozen minutes. Or was it two or three hours? Too dazed to keep a count.

The mind says, *Die!*

But the body asks, *Why?*

The neighbor's cat had sunk its teeth into the back of a young rabbit, piercing its spinal cord and paralyzing its hind legs. Creeping with its forelegs, the bleeding juvenile attempted to flee the cat. But with a single paw, the cat playfully blocked escape. Upon his approach, the cat abandoned its prey and scurried away. Arthur thought to put the rabbit out of its misery. Rock in hand, he could not rally enough courage to bash in its head. Instead, he lifted the rock high above the rabbit. He closed his eyes and released the rock, letting gravity do the dirty work. The rock flattened the fragile skull and the rabbit flatlined.

So that's the solution, he thought, as he closed his eyes. Then with a sweep of his right arm, he let the razor blade fall onto his wrist. Didn't feel a thing.

Opening his eyes, he saw only a slight incision from which oozed hardly any blood at all. He had missed a vein and, anyway, had not applied enough thrust. A bad start, but at least a start. He changed course. To open a vein, you gotta open your eyes. So now, with eyes on target, one, then a second, then a third quick stroke across the wrist. Enough to get his juices flowing, but too superficial to get much blood flowing. Ok then. This time with opened eyes and from his hand raised high above his head, he thrust the razor blade downward, and this time the blade found a vein. Gashed it more than slashed it. Bull's eye. The razor blade stood upright on its corner. He left it there for maybe a minute, or what seemed an hour, before pulling it out. He held his wrist over the sink, and blood dripped down the drain.

But why waste good paint? He grabbed a washcloth, wrapped it around his wound, and headed back to the studio, this time walking as though the balls and chains had been released. He removed the green and blue mandala painting from its easel and replaced it with a blank canvas, stretched and unprimed. A blank canvas usually presents a world of possibilities. But this blank canvas, next to none.

Dabbing a brush into his supply of dripping red "paint," and with no time to kill, he attacked the canvas with a frenzy, though usually his painting was meticulous to the point of madness. Nor was monochrome his typical style. Like late-period Franz Kline, but red rather than black. All red for now, but when the blood later curdled on the canvas, it would dry black. So like Franz Kline after all but, unlike the monstrous wall murals of the sixties, only easel-sized, not oversized. Small enough to complete in ten minutes, before he ran out of paint. Or time. Or both.

"Enough!" Arthur shouted into the suffocating air. Enough of bad paintings. Enough with painting altogether. His thoughts drifted to his reaction as a teenager to news of the death of the painter Mark Rothko.

Other star-struck teenagers at the time of Rothko's suicide were frittering away their time idolizing the latest rock star of the week. When Arthur was such an impressionable youth, his role models instead were a gang of grumpy old men draped in paint-spattered smocks whose enormous and colorful canvases filled the walls of all of the New York museums and galleries that Arthur had staked out as his hangouts.

In a dark corner of a dimly lit gallery of the prestigious Knoedler, Barnett Newman stood alone and stood out, looking portly and stately, keeping vigil over his show. Arthur overcame his usual shyness to introduce himself as an admirer of Newman's latest work. A half a year later, despite the artist's recent transformation from inert paint and canvas into living flesh and blood for Arthur, he did not grieve when he read on the front page of the New York Times *that Newman had died of a heart attack at age sixty-five.*

That same year, he read in a Times *front page article that Rothko had killed himself at age sixty-five. That death of a stranger saddened Arthur as a personal loss because Rothko no longer wanted to paint for Arthur. Rothko had had enough with painting.*

Forget the past. Forget also the future.

Retracing his path back to the bathroom, this time Arthur stepped among droplets of blood that served like Hansel and Gretel's trail of breadcrumbs in the Black Forest. But, on this return trip, the hallway must have lengthened, the balls and chains fastened again to his legs. The journey seemed to last a lifetime.

Time to hop in the shower, minus the hop. A bathtub would be more useful, but he made do with what he had. He turned on the water, rotating the lever to "hot." Still clothed, he sat down on the floor of the shower stall. The flowing water washed the blood off the wound, preventing any clotting. With every reddened drop down the drain, his life ebbed away. Tingling, he felt the harpies pecking away in his hair. Cauterizing the flow of tomorrows, the pulse in his ears resounded like the thunderous drumbeats of the timpani in the second movement of Beethoven's *Ninth*.

The Ninth Symphony's lullaby-like third movement was playing on his car stereo. Under an overcast and moonless sky past midnight, he was racing down Interstate 80 through the snow-covered and stubbled cornfields of Illinois. Sleet was falling and coating the icy asphalt. Small wonder when his car spun off the highway, slid down the sunken median between the east and westbound lanes, and plowed into a snowbank. The engine stalled, the headlights and noisy

heater fan went dead. The majestic music stopped. His heart pounded.
Except for his quickened heartbeat, silence enveloped the night.

He had survived unharmed and the car was probably undamaged.
Recovering from his momentary fright, he felt his heartbeat slacken
as he savored the moment. The quickly dropping interior temperature
numbed him, scantily clothed as he was for what he had anticipated
would be a comfortable and uneventful drive.

Frozen darkness and icy silence.

So this is Death?

The spectacle before his eyes of his blood pulsing from his vein
stirred him from his reverie. Then he looked down at the disk-shaped
drain, circular-patterned and symmetrical like his penultimate painting.
The drain's repetitive tiny black holes and the cascading water's warmth
lulled him into another memory, this from his childhood.

He had engaged in only one real fight all his life. Only one clash
of shoves and fists because he defused other arguments with talk
or simply walked away from any bully itching for a fight. He had
retreated even from those weaker than he. He was not ashamed but
rather proud of that. He refused to debase himself by sinking down
to the bully's low level.

But during this one schoolyard confrontation, a bully had struck
him on the nose. Instinctively, much to his own surprise, Arthur hit
back, his fist landing squarely on the brute's eye. The brute turned
and ran away. Triumph!

Watching him flee, Arthur felt exhilarated and glowed with
macho pride. Then he felt mucus running from his nose, over his lips,
and down his chin. Looking at his shirt, he realized it was not snot
but blood, so he forgot his unforeseen victory and thought only of the
sight of his blood.

His blood. His life was trickling down the drain. He should have
been absorbed in musings about the mysterious hereafter awaiting him.
Instead his mind flooded with more memories of his childhood.

He had been duped by his playmates. He had let his adversary in a mock swordfight choose his weapon for him. "Take the shorter stick," Judd advised, "It's better because you can get closer." Worse than Judd's deceiving him was Arthur's believing him.

Was that razor now just another short stick?

Letting that memory dissolve, he returned to the present. He fixated upon the blood trickling from his wound and then focused upon the wound itself. Now he understood how accurately the Renaissance painters depicted Christ's laceration from having been speared in the ribs during the Crucifixion. No Christ figure, he, who never found solace inside a church, least of all where an emaciated mannequin watched over the congregation. That corpse, hanging on the wall like a carcass in a butcher shop, scared the bejesus out of him as a child. Now, however, that similar wound on his own wrist provided him with some comfort.

Here he sat, nearing the end of his life with ponderings no more profound than a shopping list or utility bill. He thought not about Life and Death, concepts emphasized with pretentious capital letters, not about his own life and his own death, belittled by lower-case letters. He did not grieve over who in his absence would walk his path, would achieve his successes, conceive his thoughts, chase his dreams, cherish his memories, woo his beloveds, paint his canvases, nurture his progeny. He thought only about his wound and about his blood.

He had often found comfort in playing dead when playing war games with his childhood friends. When asked by his playmates, he volunteered to be the first cowboy tomahawked by the Injuns, or the first G.I. submachine-gunned by the Krauts. Dead, through squinting eyes, he could silently witness his friends finish the game of finishing each other off. He liked observing others play games more than when playing the games himself. Even at football, he feigned injury, so he could sit out the rest of the game and watch from the sidelines.

The chronic voyeur was now sitting out the rest of his life. Not feigning that, either. With his little remaining energy, sitting was all that he could do. Actually even sitting was an effort. Rather, he slumped against the shower wall. His hands and feet felt detached, far away, as though they too were washing down the drain. He visualized himself as viewed from without, as though his bleeding body were not in the shower but on a stage and he were in the audience, watching the drama, waiting for the curtain to fall.

A playwright can sit in the audience to watch his play, and a painter can step back to view his painting. Arthur had stepped aside to view his body, but how to step back to view his life?

His next few minutes stretched on as though for the rest of that life. His thoughts drifted away from his weakening body to the horrified person to whom was bestowed the dubious honor of dragging his dripping wet body out of the shower.

Would Todd be the one whose suspicions would lead to the discovery of an eviscerated body? Good friend though Todd was, he lived a hundred miles away. So he regularly spoke with Todd on the phone. After his third unanswered voicemail, Todd might summon the police to conduct a welfare visit.

Or would his Mom and Pop immediately grow worried by his missing their traditional Sunday-morning phone call? In which case, his folks might summon the police. Either way, a cop would discover the body, and cops at least get paid for that.

Or would Mr. Morton, his landlord with steel-gray hair and a wobbly gait, discover the corpse? A single-family brownstone stained black by time, the house had been reborn into three cramped apartments. In contrast to a feeble heart that could not outlast the weary body whose blood it pumped, the loudly rumbling boiler may have been older than the ramshackle house whose water it heated. Margie, his twenty-two-year-old neighbor with flaming red hair, had several times grumbled that his long showers deprived her of any hot water, so she would soon complain to their landlord about that lack.

Old man Morton would be involved regardless who found the body. But better to show some consideration by not dragging Margie into this mess. Most times when she greeted him, she smiled. But when complaining about his long showers, she snarled. She looked heavenly when she smiled, beastly when she snarled. Better to keep Margie smiling.

Arthur tried to raise his hand, tried to reach for the valve, tried to turn off the shower. But nothing moved. Dredged of energy, his arm, though twitching, felt like a leaden barbell, turning blue. Then all sensation became blunted. His only feeling was a shock wave of regret that convulsed his gut.

He should have waited. The body will perish within a week if deprived of food and water, so he suddenly realized that he should have simply stopped eating and drinking. He remembered that when walking indoors with muddy shoes, it's easier to take them off and wait a day for the mud to dry rather than to right away try to wipe off the mud. That only rubs it in. But too late to wait.

Water running down the drain. Tears running down his cheeks. He thought, quite a mess he's made of his life. Blood flowing down the drain. He thought, even more of a mess he's making of his death.

Arthur Kunstler wanted to wail and to scream, the way a lover does at orgasm or the way nine months later a mother might in childbirth. With his remaining strength, he could let out only a whimper, the way ninety years later a grandfather does on his deathbed. This shower stall was Arthur's sarcophagus, a gasp and a gurgle were his scream and his cry. He dropped his jaw to spout out his sorrow. Instead, water slipped past the teeth of time and disappeared down the mouth of eternity. ✳

---

*   The penultimate painting described in the opening of this chapter is real and is depicted on the back cover, just with the addition of the overlaid ghostly skeleton by Vincent van Gogh.

This chapter commemorates a true event that took place two-thirds of a lifetime ago. The names other than those of the famed Kline, Rothko, and Newman have been changed, and only its last page has been fictionalized.

In reality, Arthur has already lived to exceed the age of Mark Rothko at the time of Rothko's death. Compared to Rothko's, Arthur's self-inflicted wound was superficial, so it stopped bleeding on its own accord. Perhaps more fragile emotionally than physically, he was able to creep out of that shower to live another day, to paint another canvas, and to write another page. Indeed, many pages, including this one.

Chapter 06

Eulogies to Two Who Died Too Soon

Chapter 06

Eulogies to Two Who Died Too Soon

To Two Friends Not Forgotten

When Death comes knocking on our doors, some of us die painfully, others slowly, some suddenly, and too many die too soon. When Death beckons those we know or love, a piece of the jigsaw puzzle of our lives goes missing. Just as they have surely changed, we change with them. And after their deaths, our memories of their lives change, too.

Two friends whose sudden deaths refashioned my memories of their lives were Steve and Rynn.

Steve Ruggeri (1949–1998), Activist

Steve was our fearless leader. Without Steve, our brigade of animal rights activists would have floundered. When the news media sought someone to interview, Steve served as our eloquent spokesman on all the issues threatening to sink the ark: animal labs, factory farms, puppy mills, rodeos, whaling, trawling, trapping, and hunting. Especially hunting.

Recognizing Steve's talents, a national animal rights organization created a regional office and a paid position just for him while he continued his volunteer political and social activism with us. Three years later, he fell victim to office politics and was fired. Disheartened, Steve abruptly ended all of his advocacy on behalf of animals. He still mourned over their continued plight and over his failed past campaigns. Worse, he sulked over what he may have perceived as his failed life. Yet, none of his admirers realized that he had succumbed to chronic depression.

Years earlier, as a wayward teenager, Steve had been a licensed hunter. He shot and killed squirrels and rabbits, not many and not often. In college, he majored in philosophy, specializing in ethics. During those wakeful college years, he renounced eating animals. Later, as though to atone for his youthful indiscretions, he plotted and led our expeditions in hunt sabotage.

When the news media publicized our forays, Steve alone received death threats. He was known to be especially fond of his own dogs, so one night someone, probably a hunter, deposited a dead dog on his doorstep. For home-defense, Steve fortunately still owned a handgun, as do half of American households. After he dropped out of the movement and the public eye, he enrolled at a gun club to hone his skills as a marksman by shooting targets.

Meanwhile, our band of desperadoes scattered across the landscape. I moved to a new home in a nature preserve where in my own solitary fashion I continued our proud tradition of hunt sabotage, as though it, like hunting, had been passed down to me from my forefathers. When an article in the *Hartford Courant* spread my notoriety, hunters began directing death threats toward me. So I did what you would expect any rational, peaceful, gentle vegan to do. I took up arms in my defense.

Though long known as a social dragonfly who rarely answered or returned phone calls, Steve always returned mine. I confided to him about my new acquisition, so we talked guns. Gun owners should keep in practice, he advised, so he invited me to join him for some target practice. It being April, I suggested that we wait until the summer when I would be on vacation from my job. He agreed to phone me in June.

He never did phone me, which came as no surprise because he rarely phoned anyone. Then in July, I learned that both he and I were going to speak as panelists in September at a local conference about factory farming. His participation was heartening news to me. This would mark Steve's first engagement on behalf of animals since he had dropped out years earlier. I looked forward to seeing him in a light in which he would shine. And rather than contact him about our rendezvous for target practice, I decided to wait until I would see him in September.

Six days before the conference, Steve killed himself. He went ahead and did some shooting alone and shot himself in the head.

Since then, I no longer think much about guns, and I have almost forgotten I have one. But I still think about Steve, who I have not forgotten.

I wonder how could we, his friends and admirers, not suspect his plight? And had I pursued that shooting date with him, might his life have traversed a different course? Not that my camaraderie might have imparted upon him some new sense of self-worth. Nope, I mean something less egotistical, something far more perplexing.

Hemingway, an inveterate hunter, said that he shot animals so as not to shoot himself (even though he still ended up shooting himself). I wonder had Steve shot off his guns with me that summer, might he have blown off some steam or vented some spleen, perhaps enough to endure his depressive state past September? Maybe so, that is if Steve shot targets so as not to shoot himself. But what if? What if Steve shot himself so as not to shoot animals?

Rynn Berry (1945–2013), Author

Rynn devoted his life to chronicling and to teaching the histories and the religions and the philosophies of two perverse diets called veganism and vegetarianism. In pursuit of his contrarian goals, Rynn was an athlete and aesthete, a researcher and scholar, and a lecturer and writer and playwright. While roaming the American continents, he earned a modest living just from lecture honoraria and book royalties.

His sparkling writing edified in the manner of Emerson or Thoreau, and captivated in the manner of Hawthorne or Melville. Rynn's writing was quintessentially American, yet traditionally nineteenth century. With his unique, cursive calligraphy, he handwrote most of his correspondence with a fountain pen. Had a flight feather been surrendered voluntarily by a swan, Rynn might have written with a quill pen.

He seldom resorted to email. Unlike his colleagues, Rynn neither staked a claim to a personal website nor journaled on a blog. So don't go poking around with your cellphone looking for Rynn's writings. Google will point you virtually nowhere. Rynn shunned the internet because he hailed from the Socratic school of pedagogy. Following in the footsteps of Walt Whitman who peddled his poetry on the streets of Manhattan, Rynn mounted a virtual soapbox among the fruits and vegetables of Manhattan farmers markets. There he conversed with shoppers, lightly marketing books while stridently espousing veganism.

For his research, Rynn interviewed the living but read the dead. Among the writers who most influenced him were Leo Tolstoy, Percy Shelley, and George Bernard Shaw. Not coincidentally, they were vegetarians, and in addition to their novels, poems, and plays, all three wrote essays promoting their pioneering diets. Indeed, Rynn credited his reading Shaw with converting him to vegetarianism. Rynn was also influenced by Shelley's writings in advocacy of the raw food diet.

During one of his lectures, Rynn summarized Shelley's life as an adherent of vegetarianism, and concluded with Shelley's death as a victim of drowning. The audience was small and informal. Someone asked in jest if Shelley had been skinny-dipping. "I don't know," Rynn quipped, "but his body was naked when it washed ashore."

Our deaths provide punctuation to our lives, sometimes with conclusive periods, sometimes with question marks, sometimes with exclamation points.

Rynn was scheduled to depart on a transcontinental flight to speak at an animal rights conference, so his local friends anticipated his absence. An avid runner who twice completed the New York City marathon, Rynn set out on a routine run on the day before his flight in Prospect Park bordering his longtime residence in Brooklyn. On that bitterly cold and fateful day in late December, Rynn suffered cardiac arrest and collapsed in his tracks.

For several days, the name of the hospitalized "Prospect Park Jogger" was unknown. The only clues in his pockets were keys and an asthma inhaler. Ironically, the biographer of others was stripped of any identity of his own. In essence, his body was naked when it washed ashore.

Still more ironic, the soft-spoken gentleman of quiet demeanor who never hired a publicist nor posed for author photos to adorn his books nor queued up for media attention was now caught under the spotlights of police and framed in the viewfinders of cameras. In a campaign to identify their comatose comrade on life support in a hospital's intensive care unit, local runners clubs circulated photos of the "Prospect Park Jogger." The news media, including the *New York Times*, took notice.

Rynn never wakened in that hospital bed. When he eventually was identified, his death shined a light on his life and, intrinsic to Rynn, also upon his books, and upon the vegan diet that his books championed. But ever so briefly.

History is not the record of what has happened but of what has been written about what has happened. If no one writes it, then history vanishes. History books, too, vanish if no one publishes or reprints them. Like Walt Whitman, Rynn was mostly an indie-publisher. When I spoke with Rynn shortly before his death, we stood together behind a single table peddling books at a vegan festival. (My hustle was, "Buy two books for the price of three, and get one free.") We discussed our commerce in books. I stuck my nose into his business and advised him to contract with a larger publisher to distribute his own petite-press books.

"Otherwise, when you die, your books will die with you."

Indeed, his books went out of print soon after his death. Yet, the internet, which the author shunned, has granted his books a stay of execution, even if only temporarily. Thanks to the vast online used bookstore whose entrance doors never close, used copies of Rynn's books can still be located and bought and read. But, as used paperbacks get reused and resold and reshipped and received and reread, their bindings will crack, their covers will fray, their inks will fade, and their pages will molder. Used books that get used up soon become useless books, and disappear even from the online used book marketplace.

>All dies!
>The workman dies, and after him, the work.

>— Herman Melville,
>   from his poem, "Pontoosuce"

Chapter 07

Walking to
Our Graves

Chapter 07

Walking to Our Graves

Walking in the March of Time

The ancient Sphinx posed the question, "What animal walks on four legs at dawn, on two legs at noon, and on three legs at dusk?" Oedipus solved the riddle, for which he was anointed king. His answer? We humans. We crawl on hands and knees as infants, walk upright on our own two feet as adults, and then we hobble upon a cane or a crutch when we become old and decrepit. Or, as sanitized in euphemism, when we become senior citizens.

Bipedal locomotion is one physical feature that clearly distinguishes us from the four other members of our grand family of great apes. Yet, as we age and as our gait falters, we become no less human. Rather, our relinquishing a firm foothold and a steady pace is simply one of the many steps along life's way, albeit a step that is usually slow, painful, and among our very last.

Having been inducted into the ranks of senior citizenry, I have barely noticed its gradual and subtle steps. Deaf to the faint ticking of my biological clock, I am also blind to the wrinkles etching the familiar face that greets me every morning in my bathroom mirror. Perhaps that steamy mirror works like a facial cream that claims to eliminate only the appearance of wrinkles without claiming to actually remove them.

Museum and theater gatekeepers now grant me admission discounts, once without my even asking. Unlike my mirror, they now certify my status as an elder.

More poignantly, as my generation is now succumbing to fatal illnesses endemic to old age, the pages in my ledger of lifelong friends are dwindling. In recent issues of my college alumni magazine, obits for my fallen classmates far outnumber entries boasting the meager accomplishments of the living. My senior class has ripened into senior citizens.

If we live long enough, the infirmity and senility of old age awaits us all. Gold and silver will fill our teeth, dentures will replace our gold and silver, thinning gray hair will clog our combs and fill our sinks, wax and hair will fill our ears, age spots and wrinkles will blemish our faces. Our skin will desiccate, our gaits will slacken, our bones will fracture, our voices will falter, our hearing will dim, our eyesight will blur, our memories will fade.

Meanwhile, we march on. At the head of the parade, birth marches on. Within the parade, life beats its drums to maintain the pace of our heartbeats. And, taking up the rear, where no heartbeat can be heard, death marches on.

While we age but do not yet die, we must face the loss of those aging friends and elder family members who die ahead of us. And while we adjust to our loss of bone density and muscle mass, we learn to act our age. We no longer ski or hike or jog. Instead, we just walk. No matter how brief our action or slow our pace or short the distance, we all enlist in the March of Time.

Not yet having suffered from most of the grave health complications of aging, I do not observe the March of Time while seated on the sidelines. Whereas I have backpacked the Grand Canyon from rim to river to rim and have ascended several summits of the White Mountains' Presidential Range, I am now happy to just go for a walk down the block or along the woodland trail behind my home that lines a hillside whose downward slope is steep and rocky.

Friends beseech me to pack my cellphone when I hike my trail, warning that if I were injured and unable to summon help, I might die down there, deep in the forest. I can think of no more serene place to die.

As a tortoise ages, even its already slow pace slackens until, for one last time, it withdraws its legs and head into its shell and takes as long to die as some animals take to live. While my own tortoise-like gait is always slow and sometimes unsteady, nevertheless I walk. One of my greatest joys is walking in nature, whether the desert or a forest, whether the seashore or a city park. Walking to and from cars is at least still walking, so I enjoy walking even in parking lots. If I were able, I would certainly enjoy walking a tightrope. I probably would enjoy even walking the plank.

Modern medicine has intervened with new and remarkable ways to prolong our verticality. Whereas previously their arthritic knees landed them in wheelchairs, or their fractured hips delivered them to their graves, the elderly can now remain ambulatory thanks to joint replacement surgery. Less than twenty-four hours out of surgery for hip fractures, patients are led out of bed and instructed to walk, though for very short walks just around the hospital bed. Expressed in an idiom of the sixties and apt advice for aging hippies in or past their own sixties: Keep on truckin'.

As we creep toward that final stage along life's way, if our walking weakens and falters we can resort to mechanical aids to bolster us, our every step reenacting the Riddle of the Sphinx. First a cane, then a crutch, then two crutches, then a walker. If we become so infirm that we can walk only from bedroom to bathroom and back, that short walk will remain the one physical activity to which we will cling until the very end of our lives.

And if we continue to walk tall no matter how brief our lives, we will go walking to our graves.

List of Illustrations

About the images:
Thanks are due to all the artists and the art museums whose artworks illustrate these pages. Except for the images of Taft's monument and the Florentine skull, the museums' own websites provided these high-quality and high-resolution images. And except for the back cover painting, all the artworks have far outlived their creators, so their copyrights have long ago passed into our public domain.

on the front cover
The Three Muses
the author's montage of **Vincent van Gogh**'s three skulls listed below

the frontispiece
Florentine School
Vanitas – Skull ["*Respice Finem* / Reflect on the End"]
1520-30, oil paint on wood
Formerly the Otto Naummann Gallery, NYC

before the introduction
Paul Cézanne (1839–1906)
The Three Skulls
circa 1900, oil paint on canvas
Detroit Institute of Arts

frontispiece to chapter 01
Vincent van Gogh (1853–90)
Skull [first skull of two, F0297, JH1346]
1887, oil paint on canvas
Van Gogh Museum, Amsterdam (Vincent van Gogh Foundation)

frontispiece to chapter 02
Vincent van Gogh (1853–90)
Skull [second skull of two, F0297a, JH1347]
1887, oil paint on canvas
Van Gogh Museum, Amsterdam (Vincent van Gogh Foundation)

within chapter 02
Lorado Taft (1860–1936)
The Fountain of Time
1920, concrete
Washington Park, Chicago

within chapter 02
Paul Gauguin (1848–1903)
Where Do We Come From? What Are We? Where Are We Going?
1897-98, oil paint on canvas, 4.5x12 ft
Museum of Fine Arts, Boston

within chapter 02
Rembrandt van Rijn (1606–69)
Laughing Self-Portrait [*as Zeuxis*]
circa 1662-68, oil paint on canvas
Wallraf-Richartz Museum, Cologne

frontispiece to chapter 03
Vincent van Gogh (1853–90)
Head of a Skeleton with a Burning Cigarette
1886, oil paint on canvas
Van Gogh Museum, Amsterdam (Vincent van Gogh Foundation)

frontispiece to chapter 04
Hans Memling (1430–94)
St. John and Veronica Diptych (reverse, left half)
circa 1475, oil paint on wood
Alte Pinakothek, Munich

frontispiece to chapter 05
Arnold Böcklin (1827–1901)
Self-Portrait with Death as a Fiddler
1872, oil paint on canvas
Alte Nationalgalerie, Berlin

frontispiece to chapter 06
Hans Holbein the Younger (1497–1543)
Two Skulls in a Window Niche
circa 1520, mixed media on wood
Kunstmuseum, Basel

frontispiece to chapter 07
Hans Baldung Grien (1484–1545)
*The Three Ages of Man (*left-half panel of diptych)
1541-44, oil paint on wood
Prado Museum, Madrid

before the list of illustrations
Wilhelm Trübner (1851–1917)
Vanitas Still Life (or, *Skull on a Book*)
1869, oil paint on canvas
Museum Kunstpalast, Düsseldorf

the end piece
Andrea Previtali, called **Cordeliaghi** (1470–1528)
Memento Mori (reverse of *Portrait of a Man*)
circa 1502, oil paint on wood
Museo Poldi Pezzoli, Milan

on the back cover
Vincent van Gogh (1853–90)
Head of a Skeleton with a Burning Cigarette
1886, oil paint on canvas
Van Gogh Museum, Amsterdam (Vincent van Gogh Foundation)
   – montage with –
Mark Mathew Braunstein (1951–)
Entrance into Eternity
1973, acrylic paint on Masonite panel
collection of (if not yet estate of) the artist

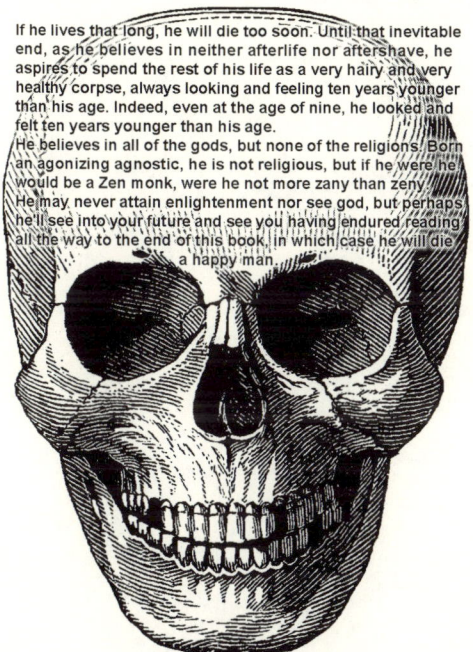

If he lives that long, he will die too soon. Until that inevitable end, as he believes in neither afterlife nor aftershave, he aspires to spend the rest of his life as a very hairy and very healthy corpse, always looking and feeling ten years younger than his age. Indeed, even at the age of nine, he looked and felt ten years younger than his age.

He believes in all of the gods, but none of the religions. Born an agonizing agnostic, he is not religious, but if he were he would be a Zen monk, were he not more zany than zeny. He may never attain enlightenment nor see god, but perhaps he'll see into your future and see you having endured reading all the way to the end of this book, in which case he will die a happy man.

The author at age 166

About the Author

Mark Mathew Braunstein walks in the March of Time on crutches. As a paraplegic since 1990, he is half-dead below the waist. And as a vegan since 1970, he is twice-alive above.

He is the author of four other propagandizing books that have exceeded their life expectancies by remaining in print even to this day. He also has scribed more than a hundred ephemeral articles in trashy consumerist magazines, most of which have since folded, and in obscure pedantic academic journals, all written with his intent to save the world, though now he is content to save his breath and his ink.

If he lives that long, he will die too soon. Until that inevitable end, he thanks the gods that he is an atheist who believes neither in an afterlife nor in aftershave, so he aspires to live out the rest of his earthly existence as a very hairy and very healthy corpse, residing with a flock of turkey vultures, another flock of wild turkeys, a herd of deer, a host of deer ticks and dog ticks, and no dogs.

Visit him at his gravesite or, if you cannot wait, at his website. www.MarkBraunstein.Org

Sleep is good, Death is better
Best of all is never to have been born.
— Heinrich Heine,
"Death and His Brother Sleep" ("Morphine")

Why did I not perish at birth,
and die as I came from the womb?
— Job 3:11, *The Old Testament*

The greatest boon is not to be
But life begun, soonest to end is best,
And to that borne from which our way began
Swiftly return.
— Sophocles, *Oedipus at Colonus*

The End

is near

no,

The End

is here